pitchers
& punches

pitchers
& punches

50 crowd-pleasing drinks!

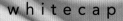

Notes

While the advice and information in this book is believed to be accurate, neither the author nor the publisher will be responsible for any injury, losses, damages, actions, proceedings, claims, demands, expenses, and costs (including legal costs) incurred or in any way arising out of following the recipes in this book.

The measure that has been used in the recipes is based on a bar jigger which is 1 oz.

The Food and Drug Administration advises that eggs should not be consumed raw. This book contains recipes made with raw eggs. It is prudent for more vulnerable people to avoid these recipes.

All recipes serve 6 unless otherwise stated.

This edition published in US and Canada by Whitecap Books.
For more information, contact Whitecap Books, 351 Lynn Avenue, North Vancouver, British Columbia, Canada, V7J 2C4
www.whitecap.ca

First published in Great Britain in 2006 by Hamlyn, a division of Octopus Publishing Group Ltd, 2–4 Heron Quays London E14 4JP

ISBN-13: 978-1-55285-751-9
ISBN-10: 1-55285-751-4

A CIP catalogue record for this book is available from the British Library

Printed and bound in China

10 9 8 7 6 5 4 3 2 1

Contents

Introduction

While beer and wine are the mainstay when it comes to party drinks, it's always far more fun when a bowl of punch or a freshly prepared pitcher of a colorful cocktail is offered instead. There's something immediately celebratory about a cocktail, and it's pretty much guaranteed to get any party off to a great start, with people gathering round while ladles of punch are transferred from bowl to glass.

Packing a Punch

Punches and cocktails have always been associated with social gatherings—the nature of these drinks means that they're perfect for sharing. It's believed that punch has its origins in India, where a specific cocktail of five ingredients, including palm liqueur and lemon, was a specialty. The recipe was subsequently adopted by sailors, who introduced the drink to seaside ports around the world.

Nowadays, many bars and pubs offer a range of cocktails and punches, and they'll often be recipes unique to the bar or involving a twist on a classic drink. These are easy to make, look great and mean you don't have to spend ages creating lots of individual drinks. Pitchers and punches are extremely versatile: whether you're cooling down on a hot summer's evening or need a warming drink in the winter, a pitcher of ice-cold cocktail or a glass of hot punch makes the perfect choice.

The beauty of both punches and cocktails is that the variations are endless and new ideas are constantly being created. The recipes in this book range from classic drinks, such as Sangria (see page 24) and Bloody Mary (see page 18), to more unusual combinations using exotic ingredients, such as Bison's Punch (see page 64) or the potent Polish Breeze (see page 16).

Basic Ingredients

There are certain ingredients that crop up in a lot of the recipes in this book, so you might want to stock up your pantry with some basics.

Mixers A variety of mixers are essential for most of the drinks in this book. Lemonade, tonic water, soda water, and ginger beer and ale are used extensively, and different fruit juices are also essential basic ingredients. When a quantity is given for topping up a drink, this is the usual size of the bottle or can and indicates the maximum amount you will need.

Ice You can't have enough ice! Don't underestimate the amount you'll need.

Fruit Lemons and limes are used most often so stock up on plenty of both. Other recipes will require a fruit decoration or slices of fruit. So, for example, the Bellini Royale (see page 27) has white peach puree as an ingredient and is decorated with peach wedges.

Herbs A lot of drinks use herbs and mint is the most popular ingredient.

Spices Many of the punch recipes include spices in their ingredients. If you have ground cinnamon and cinnamon sticks, ground nutmeg, and whole cloves in your pantry, you'll be ready to prepare most of the drinks in this book.

Alcohol The most popular spirits used in the recipes are vodka, rum, tequila, and gin, and you should also have a stock of wine, champagne, and cider. It's a good idea to pick a recipe that includes a liqueur that you enjoy anyway, so that you don't end up with lots of half bottles of unfinished alcohol in your drinks cabinet.

Essential Equipment

The great thing about creating pitchers and punches is that you don't really need any specialized equipment. The chances are that you'll have most, if not all, of it somewhere in your kitchen, and if not, you can usually improvise.

Punch Bowl Proper punch bowls look great and they generally come complete with a ladle and matching cups or glasses. However, any large serving bowl and a soup ladle will be adequate.

Pitcher or Large Jug Many of the recipes incorporate fresh fruit, herbs, ice, and other larger ingredients, and, of course, you'll also need plenty of space for the liquid.

Glasses While you can serve most drinks in wine glasses or tumblers, it adds to the visual impact if you use the right glass. The two most frequently used in this book are highball glasses, which are tall, straight-sided tumblers, and rocks glasses, also known as old-fashioned or lowball glasses, which are short tumblers. Wine glasses you

Always chop and prepare your ingredients in advance of your guests arriving and make extra— you can always store them in the refrigerator if you don't use them.

Set of Sharp Knives You'll need a medium-sized knife for larger fruit and vegetables, and a smaller one for paring fruit and chopping herbs.

Cocktail Shaker You'll find that some recipes, such as the Kentucky Cobbler (see page 38), require you to combine the basic ingredients in a cocktail shaker first and then pour into the serving jug and top up with a mixer. If you don't have one, you can just use a small bowl or jug to do this and mix the ingredients thoroughly.

Bar Spoon This is basically a long spoon that's used to stir tall drinks. It's useful for combining all the ingredients. However, you can use a wooden spoon as an alternative.

will no doubt have in any case; goblets have a shorter stem and a wider bowl. Champagne flutes are tall and slim with a narrow mouth, and their shape helps to retain the bubbles in champagne or sparkling wines, while the martini glass—the classic, V-shaped cocktail glass—is often used for serving shaken, strained drinks.

Cutting Board This is essential for cutting up fruit and other ingredients.

Pitchers

Orchard breeze

ice cubes
8 measures vodka
2 measures elderflower cordial
8 measures dry white wine
1 measure fresh lime juice
12 measures fresh apple juice
1½ cups lemonade, to top up
white grapes, apple slices, and lime wedges,
  to decorate

Fill a pitcher with ice cubes and pour over all the ingredients.
Stir well. Add grapes, apple slices, and lime wedges to
decorate. Serve in ice-filled punch glasses or cups.

Ski
breeze

ice cubes
8 measures Absolut Kurant vodka
12 measures fresh apple juice
4 cups ginger ale, to top up
raspberries and blueberries, to decorate

Fill a pitcher with ice cubes and pour over all the ingredients. Stir well. Serve in highball glasses with a long stirrer, decorated with raspberries and blueberries.

Dream of the piste as you sip on this ice-cool blackcurrant-berry cocktail

Bay breeze

ice cubes
8 measures vodka
3 cups cranberry
juice
1½ cups pineapple
juice
lime wedges, to decorate

Fill a pitcher with ice cubes and pour
over all the ingredients. Stir well. Add
lime wedges to decorate. Serve in
ice-filled highball glasses.

Polish
breeze

ice cubes
4 measures vodka
4 measures Bison Grass vodka
2 measures Krupnik
12 measures clear apple juice
4 cups cranberry juice, to top up
2 dashes of elderflower cordial
lime wedges and orange twists, to decorate

Put plenty of ice cubes in a pitcher. Build all the ingredients over the ice. Stir well. Decorate with lime wedges and orange twists. Serve in ice-filled highball glasses.

Bloody Mary

8 measures vodka
juice of 1 lemon
2 measures Worcestershire sauce
1½ teaspoons cayenne pepper
4 cups tomato juice, to top up
salt and pepper, to taste
ice cubes
strips of celery, to decorate

This timeless classic is a very personal taste, so season and spice to your preferred requirements. Mix all the ingredients together in a pitcher with plenty of ice cubes. Serve in highball glasses, decorated with strips of celery.

Sangria blanco

ice cubes
4 measures citron-flavored vodka
2 measures peach schnapps
2 measures white peach puree
1 measure fresh lemon juice
2 cups dry white wine
4 cups fresh apple juice, to top up
apple and lemon slices and lime wedges, to
decorate

Prepare well in advance of serving. Put plenty of ice cubes in a pitcher and pour over all the ingredients. Stir regularly as the cocktail chills. Serve over ice cubes in goblets, decorated with apple and lemon slices.

Long Beach
iced tea

2 measures vodka
2 measures white rum
2 measures silver tequila
2 measures gin
2 measures triple sec
2 measures fresh lime juice
ice cubes
4 cups cranberry juice, to
   top up
lime wedges, to decorate

Shake all the spirits and lime juice together with ice cubes in a cocktail shaker, then transfer to a pitcher. Top up with cranberry juice and stir well. Serve in highball glasses, decorated with lime wedges.

Arizona
breeze

ice cubes
10 measures gin
1 measure fresh lime juice
1 measure sugar syrup
3 cups cranberry juice
1½ cups fresh pink grapefruit juice
lime wedges, to decorate

This is a wonderfully aromatic version of the famous Sea Breeze. Fill a pitcher with ice cubes and add the gin, lime juice, and sugar syrup. Shake the remaining fruit juices together in a cocktail shaker to give a frothy head and pour over the top. Decorate with lime wedges. Serve in highball glasses.

Sangria

ice cubes
6 measures Spanish brandy
8 measures fresh orange juice
2 cups red wine
4 cups soda water or lemonade, to top up
orange slices and cinnamon sticks,
   to decorate

Put a small amount of ice cubes in a pitcher. Pour over the
brandy, orange juice, and wine and stir well. Add more ice, top
up with soda water or lemonade and decorate with orange
slices and cinnamon sticks. Serve in ice-filled wine goblets.

Bellini
royale

4 measures brandy
2 measures Cointreau
8 measures white peach puree
6 measures fresh orange juice
1 bottle champagne, chilled
peach wedges, to decorate

Mix the brandy, Cointreau, peach puree, and orange juice together in a medium-sized pitcher, cover and chill in the refrigerator for at least 2 hours. Stir well and serve in champagne flutes, topping up each glass with chilled champagne and decorating with peach wedges.

Pitcher perfect

ice cubes
6 measures light rum
4 measures apple schnapps
12 measures fresh apple
 juice
6 measures cranberry juice
2 cups soda water, to top up
6 dashes of orange bitters
red apple slices, to decorate

Put plenty of ice cubes in a pitcher. Pour over the rum, schnapps, and fruit juices, and top up with soda water while stirring. Add the orange bitters and stir briefly. Serve in tall highball glasses, decorated with red apple slices.

Pineapple jank

ice cubes
6 measures white rum
4 measures apricot brandy
4 cups fresh pineapple juice, to top up
2 measures fresh lemon juice
1 measure Galliano
lemon slices and long strips of pineapple,
** to decorate**

Put plenty of ice cubes in a pitcher. Pour over the rum, apricot brandy, and fruit juices and stir well. Gently pour the Galliano over the surface of the liquid so that it floats on top. Serve in highball glasses, decorated with lemon slices and pineapple strips.

Cocomo

3 measures white rum
3 measures aged rum
1 measure dark rum
1 measure coconut rum
ice cubes
4 cups fresh pineapple juice
dash of grenadine
4 dashes of Angostura bitters
cocktail cherries and orange slices,
to decorate

Shake all the rums together with ice cubes in a cocktail shaker, then transfer to a pitcher. Add the fruit juices, grenadine, and Angostura bitters and stir well. Serve in goblets, decorated with cocktail cherries and orange slices.

Spiced
mule

8 measures spiced rum
2 measures fresh lime juice
2 measures sugar syrup
ice cubes
4 cups ginger beer, to top up
lime wedges, to decorate

Shake the rum, lime juice, and sugar syrup together with ice cubes in a cocktail shaker, then transfer to a pitcher. Add more ice and top with ginger beer while stirring. Serve in ice-filled highball glasses, decorated with lime wedges.

A fragrant Caribbean twist on the Russian classic

Tangerine chill

ice cubes
6 measures light rum
4 measures Cointreau
8 measures tangerine juice
8 measures fresh pink grapefruit juice
2 measures fresh lime juice
2 measures cherry juice
1 measure fresh lemon juice
sugar syrup, to taste
lime and lemon wedges, to decorate

Put plenty of ice cubes in a pitcher. Pour over the rum, Cointreau, and fruit juices and stir well. Add sugar syrup to taste. Serve in punch glasses, decorated with lime and lemon twists, and keep chilled at all times with ice cubes.

Lynchburg
lemonade

6 measures Jack Daniels
6 measures triple sec
6 measures fresh lemon juice
ice cubes
4 cups lemonade, to top up
6 dashes of Angostura bitters
lemon slices, to decorate

Shake the whiskey, triple sec, and lemon juice together in a cocktail shaker, then transfer to an ice-filled pitcher. Top up with lemonade, then add the Angostura bitters and stir briefly. Decorate with lemon slices. Serve in ice-filled highball glasses.

Julep
shake

12 mint leaves
1 measure sugar syrup
8 measures bourbon
ice cubes
4 cups chocolate milk
sprigs of mint, to decorate

Muddle the mint leaves and sugar syrup in the base of a pitcher, then add the bourbon. Fill with ice cubes and continue to stir while adding the chocolate milk. Serve in goblets, decorated with sprigs of mint.

A frothy, chocolatey take on the classic mint julep

Kentucky cobbler

20 raspberries
12 mint leaves
2 measures sugar syrup
8 measures bourbon
ice cubes
12 measures cranberry juice
3 measures fresh lime juice
6 dashes of Angostura bitters
1½ cups lemonade, to top up
sprigs of mint, to decorate

Muddle the raspberries, mint leaves, and sugar syrup in the base of a cocktail shaker. Add the bourbon and shake briefly. Transfer to an ice-filled pitcher, add the fruit juices and Angostura bitters and top up with lemonade. Serve in highball glasses, decorated with sprigs of mint.

Pisco
highball

ice cubes
8 measures Pisco
6 measures fresh lime juice
3 measures sugar syrup
6 dashes of Angostura
**   bitters**
4 cups soda water, to top up
lime or lemon wedges, to
**   decorate**

This is a very simple, deliciously refreshing summer drink. Fill a pitcher with ice cubes. Build all the ingredients over the ice and stir well. Cover and chill in the refrigerator. Decorate with lime or lemon wedges and add more Angostura bitters, if required. Serve in highball glasses.

Bloody Maru

ice cubes
8 measures sake
1 teaspoon Japanese crushed red pepper
1–2 teaspoons wasabi, to taste
6 dashes of dark soy sauce
4 cups clamato or tomato juice, to top up
California (sushi) rolls, to decorate

A great Eastern alternative to the classic Bloody Mary. Put plenty of ice cubes in a pitcher, add all the ingredients and stir well. Serve in small china goblets, decorated with California rolls skewered on chopsticks.

Pimm's
cocktail

ice cubes
6 measures Pimm's No. 1
4 measures gin
3 cups ginger ale
1¼ cups lemonade
1 lime, segmented, blueberries, strawberries,
  and strips of cucumber
sprigs of mint, to decorate

Put plenty of ice cubes in a large pitcher. Build all the liquid
ingredients over the ice, add all the fruit and strips of cucumber
and stir until thoroughly chilled. Serve in ice-filled tumblers,
decorated with sprigs of mint.

Loretto
lemonade

ice cubes
6 measures bourbon
2 measures Midori
2 measures fresh lime juice
8 measures fresh apple juice
2 cups ginger beer, to top up
lime wheels, to decorate

Put plenty of ice cubes in a pitcher. Build the bourbon, Midori, and fruit juices over the ice, then top up with ginger beer while stirring. Serve in ice-filled rocks glasses, decorated with lime wheels.

A refreshingly tangy fizz
with a real bourbon bite

Classic
lemonade

5 measures sugar syrup
10 measures fresh lemon juice
40 measures cold water
lemon slices, to decorate

This is traditional refreshment. Mix all the ingredients together in a bowl and stir very well. Transfer to an airtight container and chill thoroughly in the refrigerator. Stir regularly and drink within 3 days of preparing. Serve in highball glasses, decorated with lemon slices.

Sweet, sharp and utterly refreshing—a hit with kids and adults alike

Strawberry
lemonade

10 strawberries, hulled
10 mint leaves
4 measures sugar syrup
4 measures fresh lemon juice
4 cups soda water, chilled, to top up
ice cubes
strawberry slices and sprigs of mint,
  to decorate

Put the strawberries, mint leaves, and sugar syrup in a blender or food processor and blend to a puree. Transfer the puree to a pitcher, add the remaining ingredients and plenty of ice cubes and stir well. Serve in goblets, decorated with strawberry slices and sprigs of mint.

Swindon
cooler

ice cubes
4 cups fresh pink grapefruit juice
4 measures fresh lime juice
8 measures lychee puree
sugar syrup, to taste
lime wedges, to decorate

A wonderfully refreshing summer juice drink. It can have a sour bite or be sweetened with the addition of sugar syrup. Put plenty of ice cubes in a pitcher, add all the ingredients and stir well. Serve in ice-filled highball glasses, decorated with lime wedges.

A dream for non-drinkers—fresh, fruity and alcohol-free

Punches

Raspberry cooler

ice cubes
15 measures vodka
6 measures raspberry puree
2 cups pineapple juice
4 measures fresh lime juice
1 cup fresh orange juice
4 cups soda water, to top up
lemon wedges, to decorate

Put plenty of ice cubes in a punch bowl. Add all the ingredients and stir well. Allow to chill, then decorate with raspberries and lemon wedges. Serve in ice-filled highball glasses.

A cool summer quencher for sipping in the sun

Petal
punch

ice cubes
1 bottle medium-sweet white wine, such as Zinfandel
4 measures Lanique Rose Petal Vodka
1½ cups cranberry juice
1 cup fresh orange juice
orange twists, lime slices, and rose petals, to decorate

Put plenty of ice cubes in a large punch bowl. Pour over all the ingredients and stir well. Decorate with orange twists, lime slices, and rose petals—try adding rose petals to ice-cube trays, topping up with water and freezing for an especially elegant decoration. Serve in punch glasses or cups.

Melody
punch

ice cubes
8 measures vodka
4 measures Malibu
2 measures Midori
2 measures coconut cream
2 measures fresh lime juice
4 cups fresh pineapple juice, to top up
balls of honeydew melon, to decorate

Put plenty of ice cubes in a punch bowl. Pour over all the
ingredients and stir well. Serve in highball glasses with a stirrer,
stirring thoroughly before serving, and decorate with balls of
honeydew melon.

Lenin's
lemonade

ice cubes
15 measures vodka
2 cups cranberry juice
3 cups lemonade
1 cup ginger ale
2 measures fresh lime juice
frozen cranberries and
lemon wheels, to decorate

Put plenty of ice cubes in a punch bowl. Pour over all the ingredients and stir well. Ladle into highball glasses and decorate with frozen cranberries and lemon slices.

Flower
power

ice cubes
12 measures vodka
8 measures cranberry juice
2 measures elderflower cordial
1 measure fresh lime juice
4 cups fresh apple juice, to top up
lime wedges, to decorate

Put plenty of ice cubes in a punch bowl. Pour over all the ingredients and stir well. Cover and chill in the refrigerator. Serve in ice-filled highball glasses and decorate with lime wedges.

Chill out and unwind with this laid-back blend

Drunk
love punch

12 raspberries
2 measures fresh lime juice
ice cubes
6 measures white peach puree
10 measures vodka
2 cans energy drink
peach and lemon wedges, to decorate

Muddle the raspberries and lime juice in the base of a pitcher
and add plenty of ice cubes. Add the peach puree and vodka
while stirring. Continue stirring while adding the energy drink.
Serve in highball glasses decorated with peach and lime wedges.

Pink, potent and hiding
a mighty energy kick

Bison's
punch

12 measures Bison Grass vodka
8 measures Mirabelle plum puree
2 cups fresh apple juice
2 cups pear juice
2 measures fresh lemon juice
4 dashes of Angostura bitters
ice cubes
lemon and apple slices, to decorate

Mix all the ingredients together in a large punch bowl. Ladle into ice-filled rocks glasses and decorate with lemon and apple slices.

A heavenly mix of plums, pears, and punchy vodka

Plymouth
punch

ice cubes
10 measures Plymouth gin
4 measures apricot brandy
8 measures fresh orange juice
6 measures fresh pink grapefruit juice
2 measures fresh lime juice
4 cups tonic water, chilled, to top up
lime slices and orange twists, to decorate

Put plenty of ice cubes in a large punch bowl. Pour over all the ingredients except the tonic water and stir well. Serve over ice cubes in highball glasses, topped up with tonic water and decorated with lime slices and orange twists.

Fish
house

ice cubes
10 measures Plymouth gin
4 measures apricot brandy
8 measures fresh orange juice
6 measures fresh pink grapefruit juice
2 measures fresh lime juice
4 cups tonic water, chilled, to top up
lemon slices, to decorate

Put plenty of ice cubes in a large punch bowl. Pour over all the
ingredients except the tonic water and stir well. Serve over ice
cubes in punch glasses, topped up with tonic water and
decorated with lemon slices.

Green Tea
punch

4 cups hot green tea
6 measures guava jelly or 4 measures guava
nectar
6 measures brandy
2 measures light rum
2 measures orange curaçao
4 measures fresh lemon juice
cinammon sticks and mint leaves, to decorate

Put the tea in a heated punch bowl. Add the guava jelly and stir until dissolved or stir in the guava nectar. Stir in the remaining ingredients and decorate with the cinnamon sticks and mint leaves. Serve in china goblets.

Royale punch

1 fresh pineapple, peeled, cored, and diced
3 sweet blood oranges, peeled and diced
2 pink grapefruits, peeled and diced
3 measures sugar syrup
20 measures Cognac
10 measures Maraschino liqueur
36 ice cubes
1 bottle champagne, chilled
orange twists and strawberries, to decorate

Muddle all the fruit and sugar syrup in the base of a large punch bowl. Stir in the Cognac and Maraschino liqueur. Cover and chill in the refrigerator for several hours, stirring regularly. Remove and strain all the fruit out, squeezing to remove the liquid. Serve in wine goblets with 3 ice cubes in each, topped up with chilled champagne and decorated with orange twists and strawberries.

Serves 12

Pilgrim punch

8 measures light rum
6 measures dark rum
2 measures pimento liqueur
4 cups fresh orange juice
3 measures fresh lime juice
6 dashes of Angostura bitters
ice cubes
orange twists and ground nutmeg, to decorate

Put all the ingredients in a punch bowl and stir well with no ice. Shake each serving together with ice cubes in a cocktail shaker, strain into martini glasses and decorate each with an orange twist and a dusting of nutmeg.

Pushcart punch

⅓ **cup melon cubes**
⅔ **cup fresh pineapple cubes**
2 lemons and 1 orange, peeled and diced
3 measures sugar syrup
2 measures fresh lemon juice
ice cubes
2 cups pineapple juice
1 cup fresh orange juice
6 measures gold rum
3 measures white rum
3 measures Maraschino liqueur
melon balls and orange slices, to decorate

Muddle all the fruit, sugar syrup, and lemon juice in the base of a large punch bowl. Add plenty of ice cubes, the remaining fruit juices, rums, and Maraschino liqueur and stir well. Serve in rocks glasses or goblets, decorated with melon balls and orange slices.

Reggae
rum punch

8 measures OP rum
2 measures strawberry
liqueur
1 measure strawberry syrup
2 measures fresh lime juice
ice cubes
8 measures pineapple juice
10 measures fresh orange
juice
cherries, pineapple and
orange slices, to decorate

Shake the rum, strawberry liqueur and syrup, and lime juice together with ice cubes in a cocktail shaker, then transfer to a punch bowl and top up with the remaining fruit juices. Serve in ice-filled highball glasses, decorated with cherries, pineapple and orange slices.

Melon
punch

1 ripe watermelon
4 cups watermelon juice
4 measures fresh lemon juice
6 measures triple sec
8 measures Bacardi Limon
4 measures Maraschino liqueur
ice cubes, to serve
lemon wheels and strawberry slices, to decorate

Slice off the top third of the watermelon and reserve. Scoop out the flesh from the remainder of the watermelon. Muddle the flesh over a punch bowl. Add the remaining ingredients and stir well. Cover and chill for 1 hour. Slice off the top of the reserved third of the watermelon and place on a platter to form a stand. Slice off the base of the watermelon shell and position on the "stand." Fill with the punch and decorate with lemon wheels and strawberry slices. Ladle into ice-filled goblets. **Serves 10**

Coco's
punch

ice cubes
4 measures white rum
4 measures aged light rum
1 measure dark rum
2 measures coconut rum
4 cups pineapple juice
6 measures fresh orange juice
dash of grenadine
dash of Angostura bitters
pineappple slices, to decorate

Put plenty of ice cubes in a punch bowl. Add all the remaining ingredients and stir until thoroughly chilled. Serve in ice-filled goblets, decorated with pineapple slices.

Planter's
punch

6 measures dark rum
4 measures light rum
3 measures orange curaçao
2 cups fresh orange juice
10 measures pineapple juice
3 measures sugar syrup
3 measures fresh lime juice
2 measures grenadine
6 dashes of Angostura bitters
ice cubes
pineapple, orange and lime slices, to decorate

Mix all the ingredients together in a large punch bowl with no ice. Shake each serving together with ice cubes in a cocktail shaker. Serve in ice-filled goblets, decorated with pineapple, orange and lime slices.

Buttered
rum punch

6 measures spiced rum
3 measures light rum
2 tablespoons butter
1 teaspoon ground cinnamon
1 teaspoon ground nutmeg
2 cloves
1 measure sugar syrup
4 cups hot strong English breakfast tea
cinnamon sticks, to decorate

Put all the ingredients in a large punch bowl and stir until the butter has melted. Serve in wine goblets, decorated with cinnamon sticks.

Egg nog

6 eggs, separated
⅔ cup sugar
1 cup heavy cream
4 cups whole milk
8 measures bourbon
8 measures spiced rum
ground nutmeg, to decorate

Beat the egg yolks in a punch bowl until they turn pale, adding half the sugar. Beat in the cream, milk, bourbon, and rum. Beat the whites with the remaining sugar in a separate bowl and fold into the yolk mixture. Serve in goblets with a sprinkling of nutmeg.

Warm up a winter party with this rich, spicy blend

Harvest
moon

8 cups medium-dry hard cider
6 star anise
6 cinnamon sticks, plus extra to decorate
6 cloves
finely pared zest of 1 orange
12 measures bourbon
1 pumpkin

Put all the ingredients except the bourbon and pumpkin in a metallic saucepan and simmer over a low heat for 1 hour. Strain the mixture into a bowl, then stir in the bourbon.

Meanwhile, slice off the top third of the pumpkin and reserve. Hollow out the remainder of the pumpkin and rinse out with cold water. Fill with the hot punch and replace the "lid" to retain the heat. Ladle into china mugs. **Serves 12**

New Orleans

ice cubes
10 measures bourbon
2 measures aged rum
6 measures Chambord
4 measures fresh lemon
  juice
4 cups cold strong black
  chamomile tea
plump raspberries, to
  decorate
crushed ice, to serve

A deep, dark and strong bowl of decadent flavors. Put plenty of ice cubes in a punch bowl. Pour over all the ingredients and stir well. Ladle into rocks glasses filled with crushed ice and decorate with raspberries.

Firetong
punch

1 bottle dry red wine
8 measures cranberry juice
2 measures sugar syrup
4 cloves
finely pared zest of 1 orange and 1 lemon
4 measures fresh orange juice
1 measure fresh lemon juice
2 measures Green Chartreuse
6 sugar cubes

Put the wine, cranberry juice, sugar syrup, cloves, and orange and lemon zests and juices in a saucepan and heat without boiling. Pour into a heatproof punch bowl. Warm the Chartreuse. Put the sugar cubes in a small metal strainer set over the punch. Drizzle half the Chartreuse over the sugar cubes, leave to soak in, then ignite. While still alight, pour over the remaining Chartreuse and leave until the sugar cubes have melted into the punch. Serve hot.

JT's Cider
nectar

1 sprig of lemon verbena
1 lemon, cut into wedges
2 measures sugar syrup
2 measures pineapple syrup
4 cups dry hard cider
4 measures medium sherry
3 measures Calvados
ice cubes
2 cups soda water, to top up
lemon wedges and mint leaves, to decorate

Muddle the lemon verbena, lemon wedges, and syrups in the base of a punch bowl. Pour over the cider, sherry, and Calvados and stir well. Add plenty of ice cubes and top up with soda water. Serve in rocks glasses or punch cups, decorated with lemon wedges and mint leaves.

Old
bishop

4 whole oranges
2 whole lemons
½ cup white sugar
2 cinnamon sticks
4 cloves
1 bottle ruby port, or you can use dry red wine

Roast the citrus fruit in a preheated oven, 350°F, for 20 minutes, then remove and place in a china bowl. Break the zest of each fruit so that the juice and flesh can absorb the flavorings and add the sugar, spices, and half the wine. Cover and chill in the refrigerator for 24 hours. Crush the fruit and add the remainder of the wine. Transfer to a saucepan and heat until simmering. Strain through a small strainer and serve steaming in wine goblets. **Serves 5**

Ginger
tea punch

4 cups water
10 orange pekoe tea bags
2 small pieces of fresh ginger root, peeled
½ cup white sugar
ice cubes
4 cups ginger ale, to top up
sprigs of mint, to decorate

Put the water in a saucepan and bring to a boil. Add the tea bags and ginger and allow to infuse for 10–15 minutes. Add the sugar and stir until dissolved. Transfer the tea mixture to a bowl, cover and chill in the refrigerator. Put plenty of ice cubes in a punch bowl. Pour over the tea mixture and top up with ginger ale. Serve in teacups, decorated with sprigs of mint.

Serves 8

Glossary

Angostura Bitters This is a concentrated flavoring that's added to many drinks and cocktails. Reputed to contain over 40 different herbs and spices, the exact combination of ingredients is a closely guarded secret. The bitters are reputed to have been originally created by a surgeon to give to flagging troops.

Bison Grass Vodka This vodka is made in Poland and, as its name suggests, incorporates bison grass—a fragrant herb that's used for medicinal purposes as well as in drinks. It's this ingredient, together with the addition of other herbs, that gives the vodka its unique flavor.

Calvados This French apple brandy originates from the Normandy region. After distillation, the brandy must be aged in oak barrels for years to develop the flavor. A number of different varieties of apple are used in the production of the brandy.

Chambord A sweet liqueur that uses raspberries as its primary flavoring. These are combined with other fruits and a touch of honey, which results in quite a thick, syrupy consistency. Chambord is added to drinks for its lush color as well as its flavor.

Clamato Juice It may sound like an odd combination, but this mixture of tomato juice and liquefied clams is a popular ingredient in a number of drinks. It's not quite as heavy as straight tomato juice and the clams add an unusual kick to a finished drink.

Coconut Cream A lot thicker in consistency than coconut milk, the cream is obtained by squeezing the actual flesh of the coconut. It's a staple ingredient in many types of Asian cuisine and adds a thick, sweet element to drinks. You won't need much and you can freeze any that you have left over in ice-cube trays.

Gomme Syrup See Sugar Syrup.

Green Chartreuse It's hard to believe that the vibrant green color of this plant-based liqueur is completely natural, but it is! If the stories are correct, just a handful of French monks know the recipe for Chartreuse, which contains over 100 different plant extracts.

Grenadine A popular drink ingredient due to its rich consistency and bright red color, grenadine is made from pomegranates and red currants.

Japanese Crushed Red Pepper Used as a seasoning in food as well as drinks, you should be able to find this in specialty Asian or Japanese markets. It will keep for a long time, so you needn't worry about wasting any that you don't use.

Krupnik This Polish honey liqueur has been produced for hundreds of years and has a vodka base. The honey provides a sweet finish and it complements more bitter flavors in drinks.

Lanique Rose Petal Vodka Another Polish vodka, this time incorporating the unusual, subtle flavor of rose petals. It has a mellow taste that should be combined with other light-flavored ingredients.

Lemon Verbena This is a fragrant herb that's used in natural remedies, cooking, and drinks. Its concentrated lemon scent and taste make it an ideal flavoring for punches, and it will complement other citrus flavors.

Maraschino Liqueur The name is slightly confusing, as this is made from Marasca, not Maraschino, cherries. The pits are also crushed and used to give an extra flavor dimension to the drink.

Midori Another fruit liqueur—this time it's honeydew melon. Midori is a perfect ingredient for summer pitchers and punches, and its reputation has spread from its native Japan to countries around the world.

Mirabelle Plum Puree This is used in various drinks, including Bison's Punch (see page 64). The Mirabelle plum is a small, round "cherry" plum, usually yellow flushed with red in color, with sweet, slightly tart-tasting flesh. If you can't find the fresh fruit, the puree is available frozen in bags.

OP Rum OP is the abbreviation for "overproof," so this is a rum with a very high alcohol content.

Orange Bitters Like Angostura, orange bitters are a concentrated flavor and are

added by the drop to drinks. Produced from the zest of unripe oranges, which is soaked in alcohol, they add a citrus kick to a variety of drinks.

Orange Pekoe Tea Bags The orange here doesn't refer to the flavor of this tea but to the variety. It's quite a strong-flavored tea with a dark color when it's brewed, so it's a good choice for other drinks that require a tea infusion.

Pimento Liqueur Also known as pimento dram, this is a rum-based Jamaican liqueur that's made from the berries of the pimento tree. It can be drunk neat or used in mixed drinks.

Pisco Pisco is a type of brandy that's made from Muscat grapes and is produced in Peru and Chile. It's used in a number of cocktails and long drinks, the most famous of which is the Pisco Sour.

Sake Sake is Japanese rice wine and it's drunk on its own, used to flavor food, and is also found in a number of drinks recipes. It's made by fermenting glutinous rice and is believed to have been

produced as far back as the third century.

Silver Tequila Silver tequila isn't aged like other varieties of tequila and is usually clear in appearance. This type of tequila is generally used in mixed drinks, whereas gold tequila is more likely to be served neat.

Spiced Rum Spiced rum is actually a liqueur that's based on rum and has various spices such as cinnamon and vanilla added to it. It works well in hot winter drinks.

Star Anise The distinctive shape of this spice gives it its name and it's usually used whole in recipes, as it looks impressive, as well as adding a rich flavor and aroma to food and drinks.

Sugar Syrup This is also called gomme syrup. If you're planning on making a number of pitcher and punch recipes, then it's a good idea to have a batch of this made up and ready to use. It's very easy to make, as you simply heat two parts sugar to one part water

over a medium heat, stirring until the sugar has dissolved. Bring to a boil and boil for a few minutes until the mixture thickens. It will keep in the refrigerator for up to 2 weeks in a tightly sealed, sterilized container.

Triple Sec Triple Sec is an orange liqueur that's a popular addition to many drinks, as it's relatively light in color and texture. Triple sec literally means "triple distilled."

Wasabi The bright green color of wasabi should give some indication of its potent taste and this thick paste is generally served as an accompaniment to sushi. However, it can also be used to flavor drinks, but only a tiny amount is required.

White Peach Puree This is a traditional ingredient in Bellini cocktails, such as Bellini Royale (see page 26), and is available in packs or jars. If you are able to find fresh white peaches, skin and pit the fruit then puree the flesh in a blender or food processor.

Index

Acknowledgments

Photography © Octopus Publishing Group/Stephen Conroy
Drinks styling Allan Gage
Props stylist Sarah Waller
Executive editor Sarah Ford
Editor Kate Tuckett
Executive art editor Karen Sawyer
Designer Janis Utton
Senior production controller Martin Croshaw